# Francis Frith's
# DARTMOOR

PHOTOGRAPHIC MEMORIES

# Francis Frith's
# DARTMOOR

◆

## Martin Dunning

First published in the United Kingdom in 2000 by
Frith Book Company Ltd

British Library Cataloguing in Publication Data

Dartmoor
Martin Dunning
ISBN 1-85937-145-0

Frith Book Company Ltd
Frith's Barn, Teffont,
Salisbury, Wiltshire SP3 5QP
Tel: +44 (0) 1722 716 376
Email: info@francisfrith.co.uk
www.francisfrith.co.uk


Printed and bound in Great Britain

***Front Cover:*** The Warren House Inn 1931  84044

*The colour-tinting is for illustrative purposes only, and is not intended to
be historically accurate*

AS WITH ANY HISTORICAL DATABASE THE FRITH ARCHIVE IS CONSTANTLY BEING
CORRECTED AND IMPROVED AND THE PUBLISHERS WOULD WELCOME INFORMATION
ON OMISSIONS OR INACCURACIES

# Contents

# FRANCIS FRITH: *Victorian Pioneer*

**FRANCIS FRITH**, Victorian founder of the world-famous photographic archive, was a complex and fascinating man. A devout Quaker and a highly successful Victorian businessman, he was both philosophical by nature and pioneering in outlook.

By 1855 Francis Frith had already established a wholesale grocery business in Liverpool, and sold it for the astonishing sum of £200,000, which is the equivalent today of over £15,000,000. Now a very rich man, he was able to indulge his passion for travel. As a child he had pored over travel books written by early explorers, and his fancy and imagination had been stirred by family holidays to the sublime mountain regions of Wales and Scotland. 'What lands of spirit-stirring and enriching scenes and places!' he had written. He was to return to these scenes of grandeur in later years to 'recapture the thousands of vivid and tender memories', but with a different purpose. Now in his thirties, and captivated by the new science of photography, Frith set out on a series of pioneering journeys to the Nile regions that occupied him from 1856 until 1860.

## INTRIGUE AND ADVENTURE

He took with him on his travels a specially-designed wicker carriage that acted as both dark-room and sleeping chamber. These far-flung journeys were packed with intrigue and adventure. In his life story, written when he was sixty-three, Frith tells of being held captive by bandits, and of fighting 'an awful midnight battle to the very point of surrender with a deadly pack of hungry, wild dogs'. Sporting flowing Arab costume, Frith arrived at Akaba by camel sixty years before Lawrence, where he encountered 'desert princes and rival sheikhs, blazing with jewel-hilted swords'.

During these extraordinary adventures he was assiduously exploring the desert regions bordering the Nile and patiently recording the antiquities and peoples with his camera. He was the first photographer to venture beyond the sixth cataract. Africa was still the mysterious 'Dark Continent', and Stanley and Livingstone's historic meeting was a decade into the future. The conditions for picture taking confound belief. He laboured for hours in his wicker dark-room in the sweltering heat of the desert, while the volatile chemicals fizzed dangerously in their trays. Often he was forced to work in remote tombs and caves where conditions were cooler. Back in London he exhibited his photographs and was 'rapturously cheered' by members of the Royal Society. His reputation as a photographer was made overnight. An eminent modern historian has likened their impact on the population of the time to that on our own generation of the first photographs taken on the surface of the moon.

## VENTURE OF A LIFE-TIME

Characteristically, Frith quickly spotted the opportunity to create a new business as a specialist publisher of photographs. He lived in an era of immense and sometimes violent change. For the poor in the early part of Victoria's reign work was a drudge and the hours long, and people had precious little free time to enjoy themselves.

Most had no transport other than a cart or gig at their disposal, and had not travelled far beyond the boundaries of their own town or village. However, by the 1870s, the railways had threaded their way across the country, and Bank Holidays and half-day Saturdays had been made obligatory by Act of Parliament. All of a sudden the ordinary working man and his family were able to enjoy days out and see a little more of the world.

With characteristic business acumen, Francis Frith foresaw that these new tourists would enjoy having souvenirs to commemorate their days out. In 1860 he married Mary Ann Rosling and set out with the intention of photographing every city, town and village in Britain. For the next thirty years he travelled the country by train and by pony and trap, producing fine photographs of seaside resorts and beauty spots that were keenly bought by millions of Victorians. These prints were painstakingly pasted into family albums and pored over during the dark nights of winter, rekindling precious memories of summer excursions.

## THE RISE OF FRITH & CO

Frith's studio was soon supplying retail shops all over the country. To meet the demand he gathered about him a small team of photographers, and published the work of independent artist-photographers of the calibre of Roger Fenton and Francis Bedford. In order to gain some understanding of the scale of Frith's business one only has to look at the catalogue issued by Frith & Co in 1886: it runs to some 670

pages, listing not only many thousands of views of the British Isles but also many photographs of most European countries, and China, Japan, the USA and Canada – note the sample page shown above from the hand-written *Frith & Co* ledgers detailing pictures taken. By 1890 Frith had created the greatest specialist photographic publishing company in the world, with over 2,000 outlets – more than the combined number that Boots and WH Smith have today! The picture on the right shows the *Frith & Co* display board at Ingleton in the Yorkshire Dales (left of window). Beautifully constructed with a mahogany frame and gilt inserts, it could display up to a dozen local scenes.

## POSTCARD BONANZA

◆◆

The ever-popular holiday postcard we know today took many years to develop. In 1870 the Post Office issued the first plain cards, with a pre-printed stamp on one face. In 1894 they allowed other publishers' cards to be sent through the mail with an attached adhesive halfpenny stamp. Demand grew rapidly, and in 1895 a new

size of postcard was permitted called the court card, but there was little room for illustration. In 1899, a year after Frith's death, a new card measuring 5.5 x 3.5 inches became the standard format, but it was not until 1902 that the divided back came into being, with address and message on one face and a full-size illustration on the other. *Frith & Co* were in the vanguard of postcard development, and Frith's sons Eustace and Cyril continued their father's monumental task, expanding the number of views offered to the public and recording more and more places in Britain, as the coasts and countryside were opened up to mass travel.

Francis Frith died in 1898 at his villa in Cannes, his great project still growing. The archive he created continued in business for another seventy years. By 1970 it contained over a third of a million pictures of 7,000 cities, towns and villages. The massive photographic record Frith has left to us stands as a living monument to a special and very remarkable man.

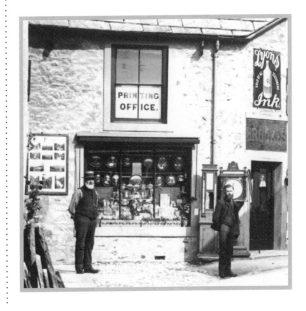

# Frith's Archive: *A Unique Legacy*

**FRANCIS FRITH'S** legacy to us today is of immense significance and value, for the magnificent archive of evocative photographs he created provides a unique record of change in 7,000 cities, towns and villages throughout Britain over a century and more. Frith and his fellow studio photographers revisited locations many times down the years to update their views, compiling for us an enthralling and colourful pageant of British life and character.

We tend to think of Frith's sepia views of Britain as nostalgic, for most of us use them to conjure up memories of places in our own lives with which we have family associations. It often makes us forget that to Francis Frith they were records of daily life as it was actually being lived in the cities, towns and villages of his day. The Victorian age was one of great and often bewildering change for ordinary people, and though the pictures evoke an impression of slower times, life was as busy and hectic as it is today.

We are fortunate that Frith was a photographer of the people, dedicated to recording the minutiae of everyday life. For it is this sheer wealth of visual data, the painstaking chronicle of changes in dress, transport, street layouts, buildings, housing, engineering and landscape that captivates us so much today. His remarkable images offer us a powerful link with the past and with the lives of our ancestors.

## TODAY'S TECHNOLOGY

Computers have now made it possible for Frith's many thousands of images to be accessed almost instantly. In the Frith archive today, each photograph is carefully 'digitised' then stored on a CD Rom. Frith archivists can locate a single photograph amongst thousands within seconds. Views can be catalogued and sorted under a variety of categories of place and content to the immediate benefit of researchers. Inexpensive reference prints can be created for them at the touch of a mouse button, and a wide range of books and other printed materials assembled and published for a wider, more general readership - in the next twelve months over a hundred Frith local history titles will be published! The

**THE FRANCIS FRITH COLLECTION**
Photographic publishers since 1860

HOME | PHOTO SEARCH | BOOKS | PORTFOLIO | GALLERY | MY CAR
Products | History | Other Collections | Contact us | Help?

your town,
your village

365,000 photographs of 7,000 towns and villages, taken between 1860 & 1970.

**The Frith Archive**
The Frith Archive is the remarkable legacy of its energetic and visionary founder. Today, the Frith archive is the only nationally important archive of its kind still in private ownership.

The Collection is world-renowned for the extraordinary quality of its images.

**The Gallery**
This month The Frith Gallery features images from "Frith's Egypt".

**News...**
**Image update complete.**
An additional 5,000 images have been added and the quality of all images has now been improved.

**Sample Chapters avaiable.**
The first selection of sample chapters from the Frith Book Co.'s extensive range is now available. All are offered in Pdf format for easy downloading and viewing.

explore
FRITH
Search thousands of photographs from one of the worlds' great archives.

Town search

County search
Select a county

**See Frith at www. francisfrith.co.uk**

day-to-day workings of the archive are very different from how they were in Francis Frith's time: imagine the herculean task of sorting through eleven tons of glass negatives as Frith had to do to locate a particular sequence of pictures! Yet the archive still prides itself on maintaining the same high standards of excellence laid down by Francis Frith, including the painstaking cataloguing and indexing of every view.

It is curious to reflect on how the internet now allows researchers in America and elsewhere greater instant access to the archive than Frith himself ever enjoyed. Many thousands of individual views can be called up on screen within seconds on one of the Frith internet sites, enabling people living continents away to revisit the streets of their ancestral home town, or view places in Britain where they have enjoyed holidays. Many overseas researchers welcome the chance to view special theme selections, such as transport, sports, costume and ancient monuments.

We are certain that Francis Frith would have heartily approved of these modern developments, for he himself was always working at the very limits of Victorian photographic technology.

## THE VALUE OF THE ARCHIVE TODAY

Because of the benefits brought by the computer, Frith's images are increasingly studied by social historians, by researchers into genealogy and ancestory, by architects, town planners, and by teachers and schoolchildren involved in local history projects. In addition, the archive offers every one of us a unique opportunity to examine the places where we and our families have lived and worked down the years. Immensely successful in Frith's own era, the archive is now, a century and more on, entering a new phase of popularity.

## THE PAST IN TUNE WITH THE FUTURE

Historians consider the Francis Frith Collection to be of prime national importance. It is the only archive of its kind remaining in private ownership and has been valued at a million pounds. However, this figure is now rapidly increasing as digital technology enables more and more people around the world to enjoy its benefits.

Francis Frith's archive is now housed in an historic timber barn in the beautiful village of Teffont in Wiltshire. Its founder would not recognize the archive office as it is today. In place of the many thousands of dusty boxes containing glass plate negatives and an all-pervading odour of photographic chemicals, there are now ranks of computer screens. He would be amazed to watch his images travelling round the world at unimaginable speeds through network and internet lines.

The archive's future is both bright and exciting. Francis Frith, with his unshakeable belief in making photographs available to the greatest number of people, would undoubtedly approve of what is being done today with his lifetime's work. His photographs, depicting our shared past, are now bringing pleasure and enlightenment to millions around the world a century and more after his death.

# DARTMOOR – *An Introduction*

SIT ATOP ONE of the high tors on a summer afternoon - Great Mis Tor, say, north of the B3357 that runs from Princetown to Tavistock. It has taken getting on for half an hour to reach the summit, for although the distance is only just over a mile the hillside climbs over 500 feet to reach the jumble of granite that makes up the tor. It has been time and distance enough to flush the city out of both lungs and mind.

Here, 1765 feet above sea level in the bleached blue of an August sky, it is possible to see many of Dartmoor's faces. North and east lie the high moors - ridges and plateaux of bleak grassland and bog fading into the distance, dotted here and there with sheep and with the dark sentinel of Fur Tor standing mysterious and lonely five miles away. The River Walkham, here little more than a brook, jinks its way through the valley past the remains of a bronze age village, visible now only in the outline of its fields and hut circles.

South-east is Princetown, hidden behind the rounded bulk of North Hessary Tor with its intrusive television mast; to the west the moors drop away to a patchwork of fields and Tavistock, nestling in the Tavy valley. South of Great Mis the Walkham continues past the ugly scar of Merrivale Quarry and drops into a deep, thickly-wooded valley on its way to join the Tavy, the Tamar, and eventually the sea.

Dartmoor's rivers radiate out from the great central plateau like the spokes of a wheel. They start as little more than wet, boggy patches which feed small streams flowing through shallow valleys, but when they reach the edge of the plateau they race off, cutting the deep and winding valleys that are so characteristic of the perimeter of the moor. South and west run the Walkham, the Tavy, the Plym and the Erme. To the north the Taw and Torridge head off through the farmlands of North Devon towards the Bristol Channel, the Teign skirts the north-east corner of the moor, and the eastern part of Dartmoor is drained by the Dart and its tributaries.

The high moors are a harsh environment, supporting little save sheep and ravens, and so the sheltered valleys hold most of Dartmoor's settlements. There are busy market towns such as Tavistock, Moretonhampstead and Ashburton - towns which were founded on the proceeds of tin mined on the hills. And there are the villages.

The great Dartmoor writer William Crossing wrote a series of articles, later published in book form, entitled 'Gems in a Granite Setting', a phrase that could hardly be bettered as a description of places like Widecombe, Lustleigh and Buckland in the Moor. Snug in their valleys, surrounded by a patchwork of fields or peeping coyly from oak woodlands, the subject of a thousand postcards and millions of holiday snaps, Dartmoor's villages are saved from being chocolate-box and twee by their functionality. True, the thatched roofs of Ponsford and the mellow granite walls dusted with the grey-green and golden lichen of centuries look great on a postcard and would make wonderful locations for a film, but little settlements like this have evolved as a practical response to the landscape in which they lie - a granite landscape, and granite is too stern a medium to allow for ostentation and frippery. The beauty of granite is better expressed in the simple lines of a farmhouse than the grandeur of a mansion.

Granite is the heart of the moor - literally. Millions of years ago, a great bubble of molten rock pushed its way up through the earth's crust and crystallised as granite. Over the millennia, the softer overlying rocks were eroded away, leaving the huge dome of Dartmoor standing proud and reaching over 2,000 feet in the north. The granite is covered with peaty, acid soils and only breaks through the surface in the form of tors - massive blocks, weathered into curious and exotic shapes. Some of the tors are surrounded by

**HAYTOR ROCKS 1927** 79779A

clitter slopes, jumbles of granite blocks strewn on the hillside, which would have been the only source of stone for the earliest inhabitants of the moor.

During the Neolithic and Bronze Ages, between 5,000 and 500 BC, the climate was kinder than it is today, and man was able to colonise the high moors. He built enclosures and feel history under your fingertips.

Man came down from the moors at some stage and began to build his settlements in the valleys, but he still ventured out onto the heights to tend his flocks and to travel, and here again he used granite. The ancient crosses that loom out of the mist are often landmarks on the routes that traversed the moor,

**Rippon Tor, The Logan Stone c1871** 5799

for his animals, huts for himself, tombs for his ancestors and stone rows and megaliths, presumably for the gods. The remains of early man's efforts are to be seen all over the moor: Grimspound is one of the best examples of a Bronze Age settlement in Europe, while Spinster's Rock near Chagford is a magnificent Neolithic Dolmen or burial chamber. The stone rows of Merrivale and Down Tor, with their imposing megaliths, are something of a mystery - were they of astrological or religious significance? No matter - touch them such as the Abbot's Way which linked the great abbeys at Buckfast and Tavistock. In addition to its use for building, Dartmoor's granite held other, more hidden riches. As the rock cooled it released vapours of various metals which condensed to form veins of ore. There were exotic metals such as tungsten, silver, arsenic and even uranium, there were copper, lead and iron - and there was tin.

Mining for tin, and later copper, was to bring something of an industrial boom to Dartmoor. Tin was worked in three phases: in early medieval times, when Plympton was a great tin port before the waste silted up the estuary, and when Chagford, Ashburton and Tavistock became Stannary Towns, allowing them to test and stamp tin; the Elizabethan period, when such luminaries as Sir Walter Raleigh held the title of Lord Warden of the Stannaries; and the Victorian boom, which saw huge quantities of ore transported along the Tavistock Canal to the River Tamar.

Dartmoor was plundered for its mineral wealth. In the south, huge pits were dug for china clay, an industry that continues today, and all over the moor granite was quarried for building stone. Tor Royal and Foggintor provided stone for the building of the prison, while King's Tor and Swell Tor quarries produced the corbel stones for London Bridge, some of which can be seen, unused, near the old Princetown railway line.

The advent of the railways gave hitherto isolated towns a link with the outside world. By the beginning of the 20th century Tavistock, Lydford and Okehampton in the west had stations, and in the east Bovey Tracey, Lustleigh and Moretonhampstead all benefited from the construction of the Teign Valley line. However, communities away from the railways were still dependent on the horse, and it was not until the arrival of the motor car that Dartmoor's last great industry took off.

Tourism is Dartmoor's lifeblood today. Widecombe, Haytor, Dartmeet, Princetown - they all play host to coachfuls of day trippers; on a busy summer Sunday the roads are crammed with cars, the occupants of which rarely stray more than a hundred yards from the safety of tarmac. Postcards are sold, probably in millions, cream teas scoffed, and the pubs do a thriving lunchtime trade. Move away from the main roads and the tourist honeypots, however, or visit the moor in winter, and a different picture emerges. Dartmoor is not merely a leisure facility; it is a living, vital land where woodlands have to be managed, dry stone walls repaired, lambing attended to and ponies and cattle rounded up. The endless cycle of life continues through the seasons and whatever the weather, for the people of the moor are not allowed the luxury of seeing it only when the sun shines. The high moor has over a hundred inches of rain a year, and Plymouth, a mere fifteen miles south of Princetown, can be basking in sunshine when the tops are shrouded in a mist that can reduce visibility to twenty yards. Snowfall and high winds can render the moor almost arctic, and while the truly great blizzards are not as common as they once were, memories persist of the vicious winters of 1947 and 1963 when farms and villages were cut off and snow lay on the ground for months.

Back at Great Mis Tor, on this shimmering summer day, winter seems unimaginable. Far towards the southern horizon the Eddystone lighthouse sits on a gunmetal sea, and to the north the blue of the Bristol Channel is just visible over the Cornish fields. A farmer, aided by four darting, crouching collies, drives a flock of sheep across the northern slope of the tor. Above, a skylark sings exuberantly as he flies, and a pair of buzzards soar, quartering the hillside in search of rabbits. Sunlight glints off the windscreen of a car as it crosses Merrivale Bridge; but here at the summit, 800 feet above the road, it seems that the 21st century has barely touched this vast and ancient landscape.

**IVYBRIDGE**
*General View 1890* 22517
In the background is the old viaduct of the South
Devon Railway, built in 1848. It was replaced by a
stone viaduct in 1893. Ivybridge Station closed in 1959
but re-opened in the 1990s.

**IVYBRIDGE, THE OLD CHURCH 1890** 22522
There was a chapel in Ivybridge from 1402, but the modern Church of St John was not built until 1882. Ivybridge did not become a parish until 1894, taking parts of the parishes of Ugborough and Ermington.

**IVYBRIDGE, THE BRIDGE C1955** 122043
The 13th-century bridge spanning the River Erme was built as a result of the increase in traffic that occurred because of the growth of nearby Plymouth. The Erme reaches the sea at Mothecombe.

**IVYBRIDGE, FROM THE RIVER C1866** 8304
Today Ivybridge has grown enormously and acts mainly as a dormitory for Plymouth, but it was once a busy market town; this paper mill on the bank of the Erme was a major employer.

**PLYM BRIDGE, THE BRIDGE AND THE RIVER 1925** 78417
Plym Bridge now lies several miles inland from the estuary, but at one time the tide reached the bridge. Centuries of silting caused by waste from tin mines on the moor were to blame.

**SOUTH BRENT**
*Church Street c1955* S360003
South Brent, on the River Avon, has a beautiful 15th-century church, St Petroc's, which has the unusual distinction of being the only church in the country apart from Canterbury Cathedral to have had its priest murdered in the church. John Hay was dragged from the sanctuary and beaten to death by Thomas Wake.

**POST BRIDGE, THE CLAPPER BRIDGE 1907** 5788

Dartmoor's clapper bridges, despite their prehistoric look, are actually medieval; they were constructed for the packhorse trains that were the transport system of the moor. The giant slabs that make up the spans can weigh up to eight tons.

**POST BRIDGE, THE CLAPPER BRIDGE c1955** D6044

Fifty years after photograph No 5788, the hillside in the background has a plantation of fir trees. The acid soils of the moor will grow few crops, but conifers thrive; the forestry industry has made the most of this, and blanketed parts of the moor with unsightly and impenetrable woodland.

**POSTBRIDGE, THE VILLAGE 1931** 83921
Postbridge takes its name from the arched bridge that was built to carry the post road from Princetown to Moretonhampstead. The bridges span the East Dart River, which rises near Whitehorse Hill on the high moors in the distance.

**POSTBRIDGE, THE OLD CLAPPER BRIDGE c1955** P102004
This view shows the massive construction of the clapper bridge; they had to be strong, as heavy rain on the moor can cause the river to rise by three or four feet and change the river from a placid brook to an impassable torrent.

**DUNNABRIDGE, THE JUDGES CHAIR 1910** 62315
The origins of the Judges Chair, sometimes called the Druids Chair (although there were no druids on the moor), are vague. One story is that it was made from slabs taken from the old Stannary Parliament at Crockern Tor, three miles away.

**DARTMEET, THE BRIDGE AND COTTAGE c1871** 5530
Dartmeet lies on an old packhorse route, which was also used by miners from Ashburton and the east of the moor to attend the Stannary Parliament which sat at Crockern Tor just north of Two Bridges.

**DARTMEET**
*The Clapper Bridge 1925*  78521
The area to the right of the river, which
here has only one car hiding coyly
behind a tree, is today the site of a big
car park and information centre; it is
rarely this quiet except in the
depths of winter.

**DARTMEET, 1925** 78513
A mile uphill from the bridge on the road to
Ashburton is the Coffin Stone, a resting place for coffin bearers on the long walk to the church at
Widecombe where funerals took place. The stone is
said to have been split in half by lightning when the
coffin of an evil man was rested there.

**DARTMEET, THE RIVER DART 1890** 25948
Dartmeet is at the confluence of the East Dart, just visible at centre left, and the West Dart. The buildings of the small hamlet remain, but the thatched house on the right has been altered greatly and now has a slate roof.

**DARTMEET, THE VILLAGE c1955** D5005
This photograph shows a much-changed settlement from that of 1871. The road is now made up, the houses have been extended, and telegraph poles are marching their way up the hill. The advent of the telephone was a real boon for Dartmoor's isolated communities, even though the overhead wires did nothing for the landscape.

**THE UPPER DART, VIEW FROM UPPER BUCKLAND DRIVE 1890** 25961
The Upper Dart flows through a magnificent wooded valley over looked by rugged outcrops such as Ausewell Rocks (just visible through the trees on the right), Bench Tor, Luckey Tor and Eagle Rock.

**THE RIVER DART, NEW BRIDGE 1890** 25954
New Bridge is the starting point for canoeists embarking on the stretch of the river known as 'The Loop' - a three-mile whitewater run downstream to Holne Bridge, tackled in winter when the river is in spate.

**WIDECOMBE IN THE MOOR, GENERAL VIEW c1955** W95038
Widecombe, probably Dartmoor's most well-known village, stands in the broad valley ('Wide Combe') of the East
Webburn river. Its famous fair takes place in Old Field on the second Tuesday in September. The first recorded fair
was a cattle fair held in 1850.

**WIDECOMBE IN THE MOOR, THE VILLAGE c1955** W95029

**WIDECOMBE IN THE MOOR, YE OLD FORGE c1955** W95012
Rural parishes such as Widecombe were reliant on the horse for far longer than their urban counterparts; the forge here was still a real forge until 1950, when the last blacksmith, Mr Prouse, closed down.

**WIDECOMBE IN THE MOOR**
*At the Village Sign 1927* 79793
Although surrounded by a patchwork of fields,
Widecombe is a real moorland village, and the skyline
is dominated by the tors: centre right is Bonehill
Rocks, to the left is Bell Tor and on the far left the
bump on the skyline is Chinkwell Tor.

**WIDECOMBE IN THE MOOR**
*The Village Sign c1940*
This sign, unveiled in 1922 as the result of a Daily Mail competition, was designed by one Joseph M Doran of Earl's Court. During World War Two all road signs were removed in the interests of security, and in the process this sign was smashed. The present sign was presented to the parish in 1948 by Francis Hamlyn.

◆

**WIDECOMBE IN THE MOOR**
*From the Moors c 1965*
This view looks west from somewhere near Bonehill Rocks. The ridge beyond Widecombe leads right out of the picture to Hamel Down and forms part of the Two Moors Way, which links Dartmoor and Exmoor.

WIDECOMBE IN THE MOOR, THE VILLAGE SIGN C1940  D6013

WIDECOMBE IN THE MOOR, FROM THE MOORS C 1965  D6101

**WIDECOMBE IN THE MOOR, THE CHURCH TOWER 1907** 5805

Widecombe is an enormous parish - some 11,000 acres - and people travel for miles to worship at the Church of St Pancras, which has become known as 'The Cathedral of the Moors'. In 1638 a thunderbolt hit the church, killing four worshippers and injuring sixty-two.

**HAYTOR, THE ROCK HOTEL 1931** 83928

The Rock Hotel still stands in the village of Haytor Vale, providing refreshment for tourists just as it once did for the local writer and eccentric Beatrice Chase. The author of many romantic works about the moor, she took the title of 'My Lady of the Moor' bestowed on her by an admirer.

**HAYTOR, THE ROCKS 1927** 79779A
Haytor Rocks stand on one side of a broad grassy
avenue. Opposite is Low Man, the west face of which is
the highest cliff on the moor at 130 feet. One local
claims that in the winter of 1963 the snowdrifts at Low
Man were so deep he tobogganed off the top!

**HAYTOR 1927** 79777
This is a favourite spot today for tourists because of its height (457 metres) and the panoramic views as far as Portland in the east and The Lizard in the south-west. In the 19th century Haytor was more likely to be frequented by quarrymen working the granite quarries on the other side of the hill.

**HAYTOR, MOORLAND ROAD TO WIDECOMBE 1920** 69622
In 1975 Devon County Council bought Haytor Rock and Down - all 1085 acres of it - for just £15,000. Where the road meets the horizon is now a large car park, haunt of coaches and ice cream vans - and a great place for kite flying.

**HAYTOR, THE MOORLAND HOTEL 1908** 56584
On 6 March 1970, sixty firemen fought a fierce blaze here. 250 guests attending a ball had to be evacuated, and most of the upper storey was destroyed.

**RIPPON TOR, THE LOGAN STONE c1871** 5799

There used to be several of these improbably-balanced natural rock formations on the moor. They could be rocked to and fro quite easily, and this one was known as the Nutcracker, for obvious reasons. It fell prey to vandals in the 1970s.

**PONSWORTHY, THE SPLASH c1960** D6142

Hiding in the valley of the West Webburn River, which eventually joins the East Webburn and flows into the Dart, Ponsworthy is one of the moor's most attractive hamlets. The Splash is a ford where a tributary stream flows over the road.

**GRIMSPOUND 1922** 73161

Grimspound, a few miles north of Widecombe, is one of the finest examples of a Bronze Age village in Europe. It lies half a mile off the road to the right. On the horizon is Hookney Tor.

**THE RIVER DART, HOLNE BRIDGE 1890** 25949

The 15th-century bridge at Holne spans a deep pool in the river; it has become a popular spot for the time-honoured pastime of bridge-jumping, usually undertaken after some minutes spent teetering on the parapet with pulse racing!

**ASHBURTON**
*North Street 1890* 25944
Ashburton lies on the River Ashburn, and was declared a Stannary Town in 1285 by Edward I. This allowed the official testing and stamping of tin, which contributed greatly to the town's wealth and also to the exchequer through Coinage Duty.

**ASHBURTON, NORTH STREET 1904** 51203
The fine granite Market Hall (left) was built by Lord Clinton in 1850; the old Market House in the Bull Ring had been demolished on his orders two years previously.

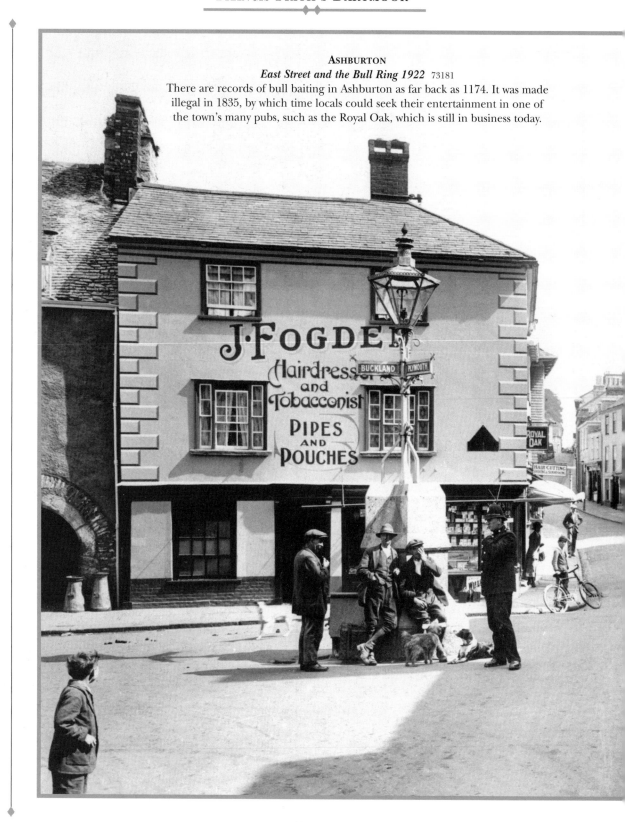

**ASHBURTON**
*East Street and the Bull Ring 1922* 73181
There are records of bull baiting in Ashburton as far back as 1174. It was made illegal in 1835, by which time locals could seek their entertainment in one of the town's many pubs, such as the Royal Oak, which is still in business today.

ASHBURTON
*North Street 1922* 73180
Some of the kerbstones which line Ashburton's narrow
streets are made from fine pink marble, quarried
locally. At one point they were nearly removed during
a road improvement scheme, but prompt action by
the locals preserved them.

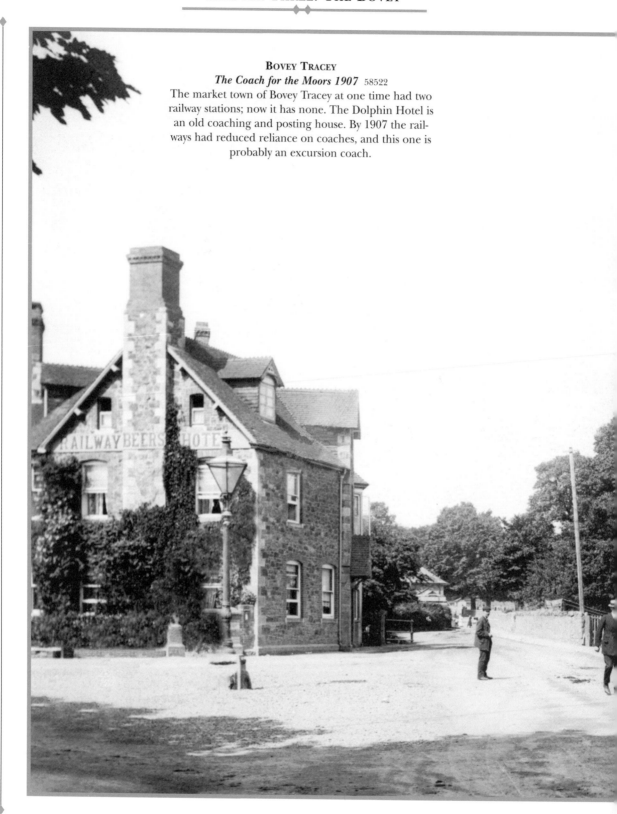

**BOVEY TRACEY**
*The Coach for the Moors 1907* 58522
The market town of Bovey Tracey at one time had two
railway stations; now it has none. The Dolphin Hotel is
an old coaching and posting house. By 1907 the railways had reduced reliance on coaches, and this one is
probably an excursion coach.

**LUSTLEIGH CLEAVE, FROM THE EAST c1871** 5811
Lustleigh Cleave, one of the Moor's most scenic valleys, lies to the west of Lustleigh itself and was cut by the River Bovey. This view is probably from Sharpitor, one of the many rocky outcrops that dot the northern side of the Cleave.

**LUSTLEIGH, AN OLD COTTAGE 1906** 56596
Lustleigh is a showpiece still of the thatcher's art. West country thatching is done with straw, rather than the reed that is used in other parts of the country, but the tools are much the same - iron hooks, hand shears, shearing hook, sparhook and leggat.

**LUSTLEIGH, THE VILLAGE 1907** 58444
It is high summer; just the weather for relaxing on the parapet of the little bridge that spans the Wray Brook, which eventually flows into the River Bovey just downstream from Drakeford Bridge. The dog seems glad of the shade.

LUSTLEIGH
*From the East 1920  69626*

This is an idyllic scene - horses no longer work the land now, but as late as 1987 they were being used by the National Park Authority in woodlands near Moretonhampstead. Just visible in the centre of the picture is the Teign Valley railway line which used to run to Moretonhampstead.

**LUSTLEIGH, THE VILLAGE c1960** L115027

**LUSTLEIGH**
*The Village c1960*
The Church of St John the Baptist's
most eccentric incumbent was the Rev
William Davy (1743-1826), who printed
26 volumes of his 'System of Divinity'
(unreadable, apparently, although you
are welcome to try if you can find a
copy) and followed it up with a mere six
volumes of collected sermons. Neither
made the best-seller list.

**BECKY FALLS 1922**
The valley through which Becka Brook
flows is typical of the valleys on the edge
of the moor - dense oak woodland,
home to many species of birds including
the scarce pied flycatcher, and with the
boulders in the river bed thickly fes-
tooned with bright green moss.

**BECKY FALLS 1922** 73158

**MANATON, VIEW ON THE OLD MANATON ROAD 1907** 58459
A view which shows just how remote settlements such as Manaton would have been in the days before the motor car - although only eight miles from Bovey Tracey, the deep wooded valleys, bleak moorland hills and rough tracks would have made the journey something of an expedition.

**MANATON, THE MOORS C1955** M20016
Manaton is on the valley side above Hayne Brook, which joins the Bovey via Becka Brook. Milk churns such as those here are no longer seen - milk is now collected by tanker.

**MANATON, THE CHURCH 1907** 58460
This was the scene of a devastating lightning strike on 13 December 1779. The east front of the chancel was demolished (perhaps explaining the new roof tiles on the right) and the north side of the tower was split almost to the ground. 'In short a sight shocking to all beholders' (Manaton Parish Register).

**MORETONHAMPSTEAD, GENERAL VIEW 1931** 84050
Moretonhampstead stands on the watershed between the Teign and Bovey Rivers. In the Domesday Book its name is recorded as Mortona, and it was later known as Mor Tun; locals still refer to it as Moreton. Prominent on the horizon (right) are Haytor and Low Man.

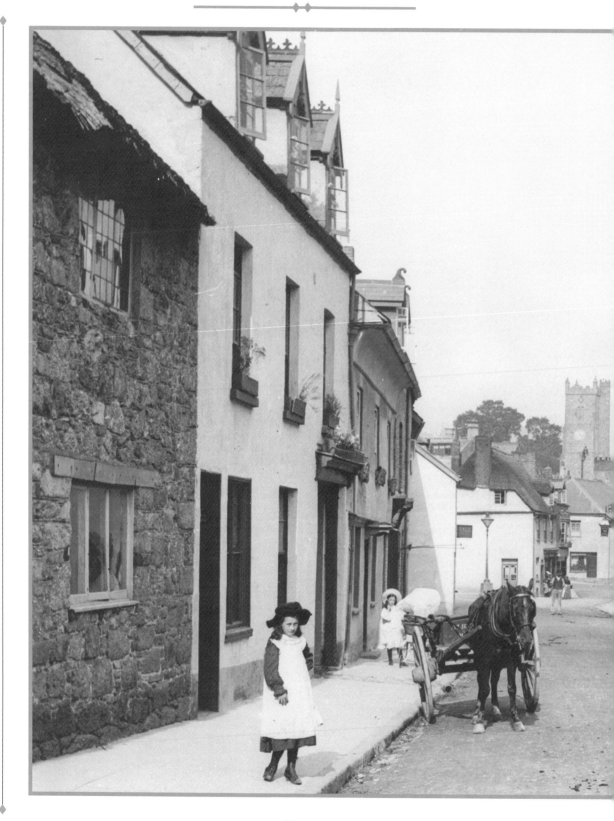

**MORETONHAMPSTEAD**
*Court Street 1906* 56602

Cross Street was the scene of a great fire which began in a bakehouse on 12 September 1845. Forty houses and several shops were destroyed. Other fires occurred in 1803, 1816, 1838 and 1926.

**MORETONHAMPSTEAD**
*The Sentry 1918* 68599
The Sentry is the name given to the hillside in front of the church, which commands good views of the southern approaches to Moretonhampstead. Stooks of corn like those in this picture have faded into countryside memory.

**MORETONHAMPSTEAD, CHURCH STREET 1906** 56604
The Church of St Andrew, with its fine Gothic granite tower, dates from around 1418. On the right a wheelwright is going about his trade.

**MORETONHAMPSTEAD, CROSS STREET c1960** M97012
The White Hart Hotel was the venue for the last Stannary Parliament to be held on Dartmoor on 11 December 1786. The practice of holding the Parliament at Crockern Tor, 1,200 feet up in the middle of the moor, had very sensibly ceased some time before.

**MORETONHAMPSTEAD, THE CHURCH c1960** M97018
During the Napoleonic Wars, French officers lived on parole in Moretonhampstead, occasionally gathering around the Cross Tree to give a concert. Two of them are buried in the churchyard.

**DREWSTEIGHNTON, FINGLE BRIDGE c1960** D85011
Fingle Bridge, typical of an old Dartmoor pack bridge, spans the River Teign. On the right is The Angler's Rest and behind it Prestonbury Hill, on top of which is the prehistoric Prestonbury Fort.

**DREWSTEIGNTON, FINGLE BRIDGE c1960** D85001
The Teign is a great sea trout river, much fished by the likes of the Rev Richard Peak, a 19th-century Rector of Drewsteignton who spent as much time casting the fly as he did looking after his flock.

**DREWSTEIGNTON, THE CHURCH c1960** D85002
The Church of the Holy Trinity was built in the 15th and 16th centuries, and the chancel was rebuilt in 1863. On the left is the Drew Arms, which had one of the longest-serving landladies in the country - Aunt Mabel Mudge, who held the licence for over 60 years.

**FINGLE GLEN AND THE RIVER TEIGN 1910** 62444
This photograph was taken from the eastern end of the glen, two miles upstream from Fingle Bridge. The cliff in the centre is Sharp Tor which, unusually for Dartmoor, is shale rather than granite.

### CHAGFORD

*Market Place 1906* 56609

Chagford's striking octagonal Market House was built in
1862. An earlier Market House collapsed in 1618, killing
ten people who were attending the Stannary Court.
Chagford was declared one of the first Devon Stannary
towns in 1305, but by the late 16th century the tin was
worked out and the town turned to spinning wool.

**CHAGFORD, THE THREE CROWNS 1922** 73126
The porch of the Three Crowns was the scene in 1643 of the shooting during a skirmish with Parliamentarian forces of the Royalist poet Sidney Godolphin, described by a contemporary as 'perfect and as absolute a piece of virtue as ever our nation bred'.

**CHAGFORD, RUSHFORD BRIDGE 1907** 58475
Rushford Bridge lies north of Chagford on the River Teign. A mile upstream is Chagford Bridge, site of the ford from which the town takes its name - 'chag' is the Old English for gorse or broom. The first bridge there was built in 1244.

### CHAGFORD
*The Square 1922* 73124

Practical Dartmoor politics: 'Chagford residents - will all residents interested in the suggestion of Yellow Lines parade in Chagford Square at 11 till
11.15am on Saturday, 10 May. Those in favour are invited to stand in the
centre of the Square and those against to stand on the peripheral pave-
ments. Our elected councillors can thus be shown what the electors want'.
Personal column in The Western Morning News, 2 May 1969.

**CHAGFORD, LOOKING DOWN MILL STREET 1922** 73125A
Mill Street is named after the blanket and serge mill opened in the early 18th century by a Mr Berry, whose town house is now the Moorlands Hotel.

**CHAGFORD, THE GLOBE HOTEL 1931** 83907
The Globe Hotel was originally a post house. The London and South Western Railway used to pick up here for Exeter railway station.

**OKEHAMPTON**
*Fore Street Market 1890* 22590
The Town Hall (left) was built in 1685 by John
Northmore as a private house and converted in 1821.
Okehampton received its charter in 1623 and until
1832 sent two MPs to Parliament.

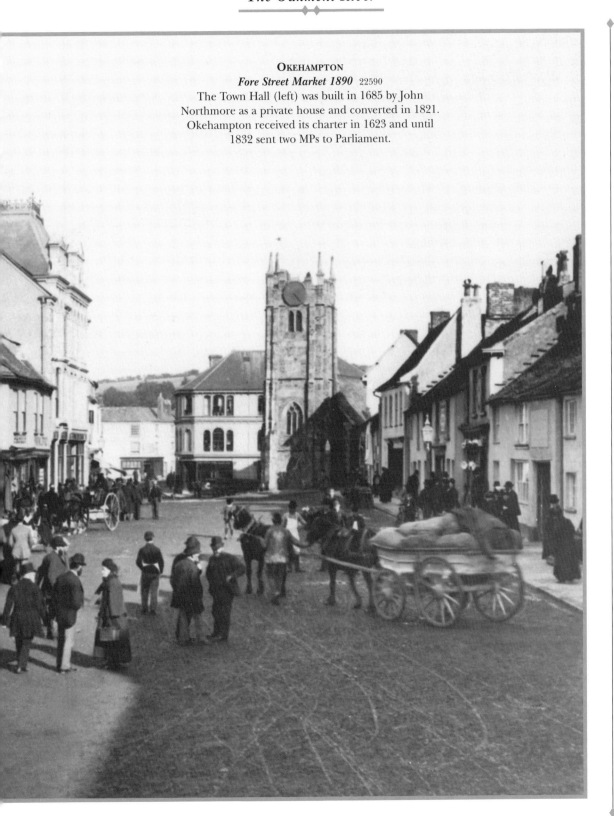

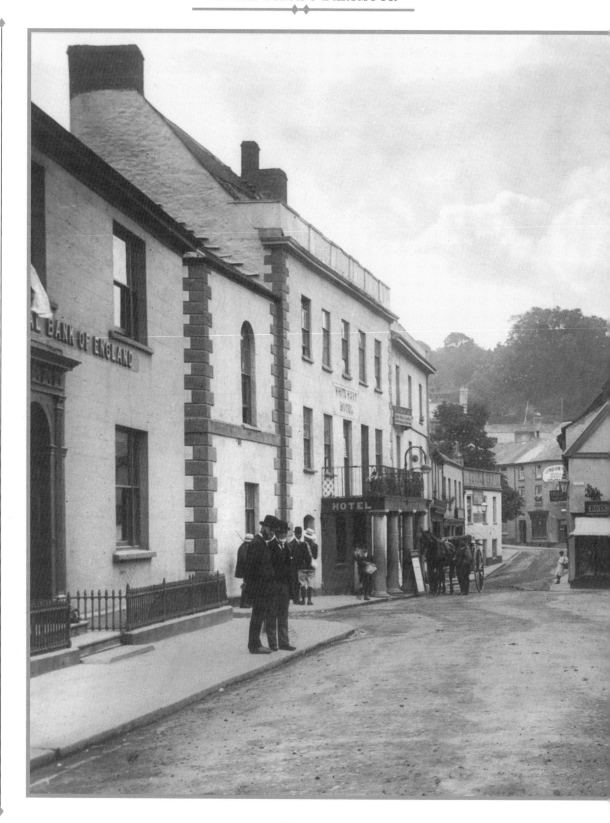

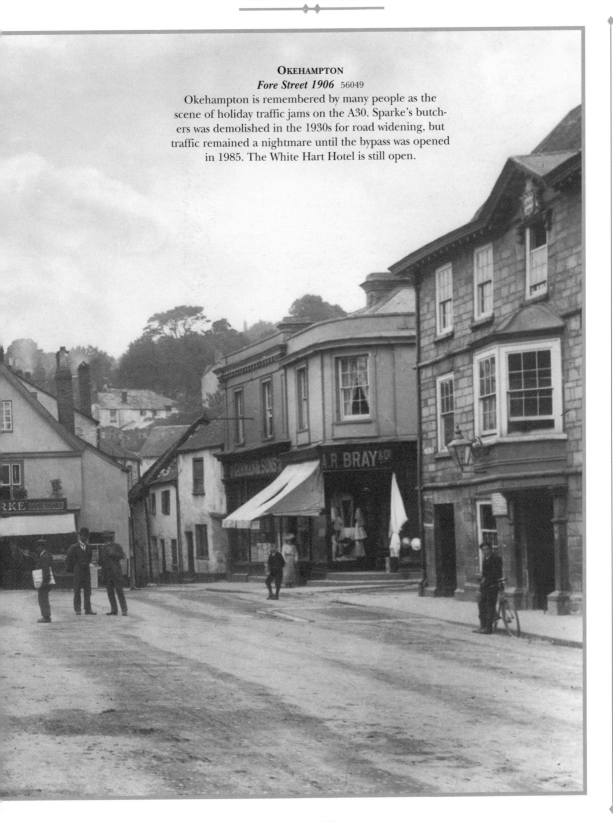

**OKEHAMPTON**
*Fore Street 1906* 56049
Okehampton is remembered by many people as the
scene of holiday traffic jams on the A30. Sparke's butch-
ers was demolished in the 1930s for road widening, but
traffic remained a nightmare until the bypass was opened
in 1985. The White Hart Hotel is still open.

**OKEHAMPTON, FORE STREET c1871** 5765
The main church of Okehampton is a little way out of town; the one in this picture is the Chantry Chapel of St James. The tower was built in the 15th century, and the rest was rebuilt in 1862.

**OKEHAMPTON, THE CASTLE 1890** 22589
Okehampton was founded by Baldwin de Brionne, Norman Sheriff of Devon in 1086. The Norman keep of the castle dates from around that time, the rest is 13th-century.

**OKEHAMPTON, MELDON VIADUCT 1906** 56058
The viaduct was built in 1874 over the West Okement River to carry the Lydford Junction to Okehampton line. It spans 561 feet and is 150 feet high. The upper part of the valley now holds Meldon Reservoir.

**LYDFORD, THE RIVER LYD AND BRAT TOR 1922** 73176
The River Lyd rises high on the moor near Woodcock Hill and eventually joins the Tamar near Lifton. Lydford was a Saxon Mint Town and a seat of power under Alfred the Great.

**LYDFORD, THE CASTLE 1906** 56070
The Castle was built in 1195 to supersede the previous earthworks. The castle dungeon was used as the Stannary Prison, although Lydford never had the status of Stannary Town.

**LYDFORD, THE VILLAGE AND THE TORS 1907** 57508

This photograph was taken from the tower of the 15th-century church of St Petroc. In the distance are the western hills of the moor, culminating at the prominent nipple of Yes Tor (2028 feet) just left of centre.

**THE GORGE, LYDFORD c1955** D6096

Lydford's famous gorge was in the 17th century home to a gang of red-bearded ruffians called the Gubbins, who terrorised the locals before dying 'as a result of intemperance and interbreeding'.

## LYDFORD
### *The Railway Junction 1907* 57503
The London and South Western Railway arrived from Tavistock in 1865, and the line to Okehampton was completed in 1874. The last train on the line ran on 6 May 1968.

**MARY TAVY, ELLIOTS HOTEL 1908** 59741
Elliots Hotel became the Bullers Arms before taking the name it has today - The Mary Tavy Inn. Two miles north of Mary Tavy is Wheal Betsy, one of Dartmoor's most famous mines; in the middle of the 19th century it was producing over 1,000 tons of lead and 2,000 ounces of silver annually.

**TAVISTOCK**
*General View 1893* 32113

Tavistock, one of Devon's three original Stannary Towns, lies on the banks of the Tavy, which rises high on the moors near Cut Hill and flows into the Tamar upstream of Tamerton. In the background is the viaduct of the Okehampton railway line.

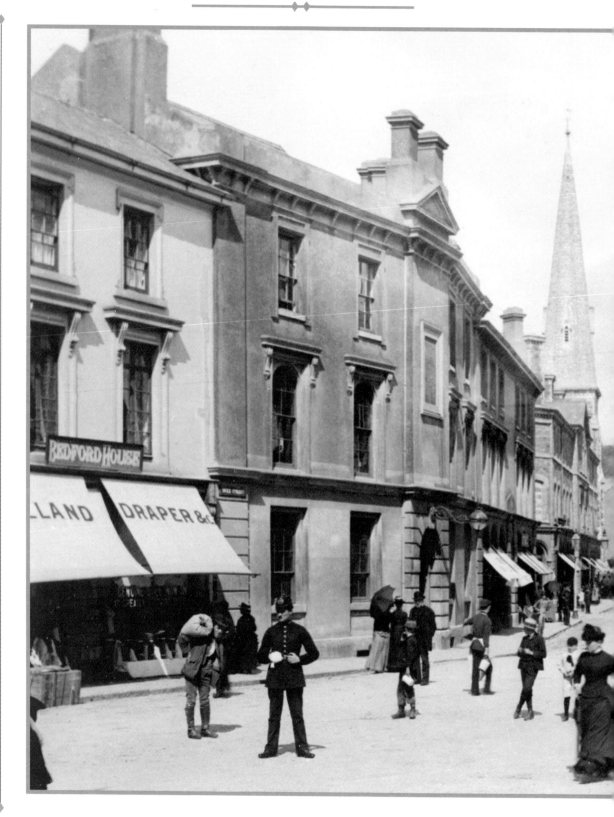

**TAVISTOCK**
*Duke Street 1890* 22546
The name of Bedford can be seen all round Tavistock (Bedford House, right, and Bedford Square, left). The Dukes of Bedford were granted Tavistock Abbey and its lands at the dissolution of the monasteries by Henry VIII.

**TAVISTOCK**
*Duke Street 1910* 62256
The ivied building on the right is the Congregational
Church, built in 1873. Its graceful spire was a promi-
nent landmark until it was demolished in 1960.

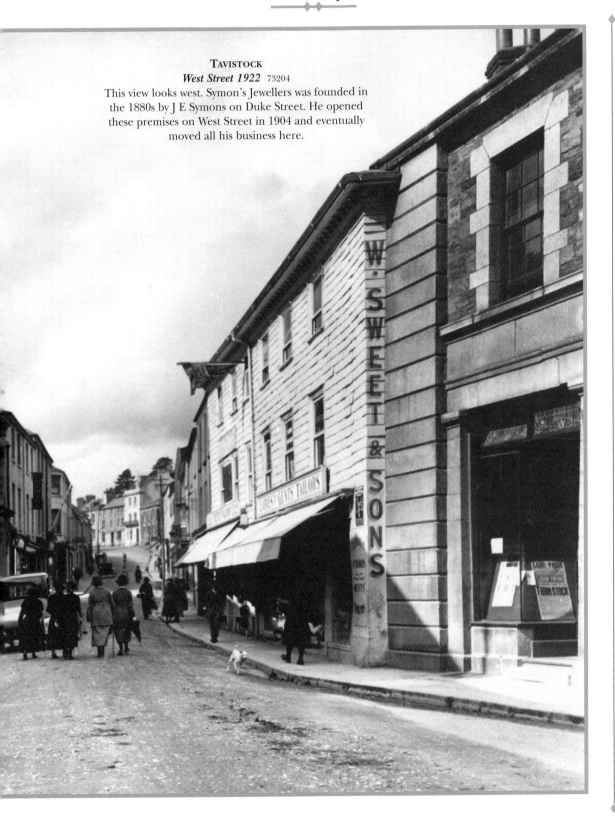

**TAVISTOCK**
*West Street 1922* 73204
This view looks west. Symon's Jewellers was founded in
the 1880s by J E Symons on Duke Street. He opened
these premises on West Street in 1904 and eventually
moved all his business here.

**TAVISTOCK, ST EUSTACE CHURCH 1934** 86030
Tavistock's parish church, St Eustachius, was originally dedicated in 1318, commemorating two Roman martyrs. It was rebuilt in the 15th century.

**TAVISTOCK, THE GUILDHALL 1893** 32118
Construction of the Guildhall was commenced in 1848 on the orders of the 7th Duke, whose statue stands in front. It was completed in 1864. As well as filling the usual civic functions, it was also the Police Station and the home of the fire engine.

**TAVISTOCK, THE BEDFORD HOTEL 1893** 32120
The hotel was originally the Abbey House, but was converted to a hotel in 1822. The low building is the Bedford estate office. Tavistock's Goose fair is held in Bedford Square on the second Wednesday in October.

**TAVISTOCK, ABBEY BRIDGE 1896** 38914
Abbey Bridge was built in 1763 to carry the turnpike road to Plymouth. It was widened in 1860 to give access to the Great Western Railway station. The weir was destroyed in a flood in 1890 and rebuilt.

**MERRIVALE, BRIDGE 1910** 62321
Merrivale Bridge crosses the Walkham, which rises in the centre of the high moors. This old bridge still stands, but the Princetown to Tavistock road now takes a newer bridge alongside.

**MERRIVALE, BRIDGE 1910** 62319
In the background is Merrivale Quarry, granite from which has been used in many famous structures including London Bridge, now in Arizona. The quarry cottages are long gone, but the Dartmoor Inn (centre) is a popular watering-hole still.

**WALKHAMPTON**
*Huckworthy Bridge 1910*  62289
Walkhampton is an old (the name is
recorded as early as 1083) and huge
parish, taking in the high moors as far
east as Eylesbarrow. The bridge
was built in 1842.

**HORRABRIDGE**
*The Bridge 1898* 42244
There has been a bridge here since the 11th century.
Recent roadworks revealed within the existing struc-
ture a much earlier bridge, possibly medieval, around
which the present bridge was built.

**HORRABRIDGE, THE BRIDGE 1898** 42243

Upstream (right) of the bridge is a weir, at which it is possible to see salmon leaping. The Leaping Salmon Inn is downstream of the bridge on the other side of the river, and the house with the white curtains at the end of the terrace is a newsagent and general store.

**YELVERTON, THE VILLAGE c1965** Y10028

This part of Yelverton, separated from the rest of the village by the main road, goes by the curious name of Leg O'Mutton. The Midland Bank, now HSBC, still opens three days a week, and the cafe on the left is now a hairdressers.

**YELVERTON, THE HOTEL c1955** Y10021

The Yelverton Hotel is now the Leg O'Mutton, and the flat-roofed building beyond is today home to the Walkham Gallery and a haberdashers. The garage is still open, but no longer sells petrol.

**YELVERTON**
*Roborough Rocks 1898*  42255
The rocks stand at the end of what was during World War Two the runway of RAF Harrowbeer, so called because of worries that 'RAF Yelverton' might sound too much like 'RAF Yeovilton' on the crackly radio of a Spitfire or Hurricane. The rocks were lowered by several feet to prevent planes flying into them.

**YELVERTON, THE PARADE 1934** 86251
The large villas are now gone, replaced by flat-roofed shops, estate agents and banks. The Rock Hotel garage, visible left of the tree in the background, is now a beauty clinic, but the Rock Inn remains, hidden behind the tree.

**PRINCETOWN**
*Dartmoor Prison 1890* 22574
Princetown is an unlikely spot for a town - 1400 feet
above sea level, on an exposed col between North
Hessary Tor (top left, without the TV mast that adorns
it today) and South Hessary Tor, and with an annual
rainfall between 80-100 inches.

**PRINCETOWN, DARTMOOR PRISON c1898** 41952

Princetown owes its existence to Sir Thomas Tyrwhitt, Lord Warden of the Stannaries, who needed men to work his granite quarries nearby; to this end he built the Tavistock to Princetown road and was instrumental in the building of the prison.

**PRINCETOWN, DARTMOOR PRISON c1955** P115017

The prison was built to house French prisoners from the Napoleonic Wars, the first of whom (2,500 of them) arrived on 24 May 1809. The prison population eventually reached 9,000, but when the war ended in 1816 the prison closed.

**PRINCETOWN, DARTMOOR PRISON c1965** P115028
The prison was re-opened and greatly extended in 1850, and was used to house criminals rather than prisoners of war. Its isolation made it ideal for incarcerating the most hardened villains, and it became one of the most notorious penal institutions in the world.

**PRINCETOWN,**
*Dartmoor Prison Gate and Convicts 1890*
22578

The prison regime was harsh; convicts were often harnessed to haul carts, and most spent their time breaking rocks in the quarries in the severe Dartmoor climate. Beatings and floggings were common, and strait-jackets, leg-irons and the ball and chain were all used. Not for nothing was it known as 'Halfway to Hell'

**PRINCETOWN, THE ENTRANCE, DARTMOOR PRISON c1965** P115031
By the 1960s the regime had softened, partly as a result of the great mutiny of 1932, but some hard characters still resided here. Frank 'The Axeman' Mitchell, according to local lore, used to walk the moors on parole before he was sprung by the Krays, who subsequently bumped him off.

**PRINCETOWN**
*Tavistock Road 1931*  84058
A somewhat macabre tourist industry sprung up around the prison, with charabancs bringing
people from far and wide to gawp at 7 Tor View, Princetown - the prison's postal address.

**PRINCETOWN, TAVISTOCK ROAD 1935** 86939
This photograph was taken from near the old Prison Officers' Mess, now the Dartmoor National Park Information Centre. Lord's Cafe is still in business.

**PRINCETOWN, TAVISTOCK ROAD c1955** P115005

In the background on the left is the Church of St Michael, the only one in the world to have been built and decorated by prisoners of war. It was completed in 1813, and the first service was held on 2 January 1814.

**PRINCETOWN, TAVISTOCK ROAD c1955** P115006

The Plume of Feathers Hotel is one of Dartmoor's busiest hostelries and a waypoint for walkers. It lies on the Abbot's Way, the old track that linked the Abbeys at Tavistock and Buckfast.

**PRINCETOWN, THE GREEN c1955** P115007

The Railway Hotel (background) was built for travellers on the railway, which arrived in 1883. Although a lifeline for the village, the railway always had financial problems and closed in 1956.

**PRINCETOWN, DARTMOOR PONIES c1965** P115024

The Railway Hotel is now the Devil's Elbow, a name taken from a notorious kink in the road a mile to the south which was the scene of many accidents and heart-stopping moments. It was straightened out in 1964, thus rendering the journey rather less exciting.

**THE WARREN HOUSE INN 1931** 84044
The Warren House Inn, at over 1400 feet above sea level, has the distinction of being the highest pub in Devon and one of the highest in the country. It stands at the side of the road between Two Bridges and Moretonhampstead.

**THE WARREN HOUSE INN 1931** 84046
The Warren House Inn has another unusual claim to fame - the fire there has never gone out since it was built in 1845 to replace another inn on the opposite side of the road.

# Index

# Frith Book Co Titles

## www.francisfrith.co.uk

The Frith Book Company publishes over 100 new titles each year. A selection of those currently available is listed below. For latest catalogue please contact Frith Book Co.
**Town Books** 96 pages, approximately 100 photos. **County and Themed Books** 128 pages, approximately 150 photos (unless specified). All titles hardback with laminated case and jacket, except those indicated pb (paperback)

| | | | | | |
|---|---|---|---|---|---|
| Amersham, Chesham & Rickmansworth (pb) | 1-85937-340-2 | £9.99 | Devon (pb) | 1-85937-297-x | £9.99 |
| Andover (pb) | 1-85937-292-9 | £9.99 | Devon Churches (pb) | 1-85937-250-3 | £9.99 |
| Aylesbury (pb) | 1-85937-227-9 | £9.99 | Dorchester (pb) | 1-85937-307-0 | £9.99 |
| Barnstaple (pb) | 1-85937-300-3 | £9.99 | Dorset (pb) | 1-85937-269-4 | £9.99 |
| Basildon Living Memories (pb) | 1-85937-515-4 | £9.99 | Dorset Coast (pb) | 1-85937-299-6 | £9.99 |
| Bath (pb) | 1-85937-419-0 | £9.99 | Dorset Living Memories (pb) | 1-85937-584-7 | £9.99 |
| Bedford (pb) | 1-85937-205-8 | £9.99 | Down the Severn (pb) | 1-85937-560-x | £9.99 |
| Bedfordshire Living Memories | 1-85937-513-8 | £14.99 | Down The Thames (pb) | 1-85937-278-3 | £9.99 |
| Belfast (pb) | 1-85937-303-8 | £9.99 | Down the Trent | 1-85937-311-9 | £14.99 |
| Berkshire (pb) | 1-85937-191-4 | £9.99 | East Anglia (pb) | 1-85937-265-1 | £9.99 |
| Berkshire Churches | 1-85937-170-1 | £17.99 | East Grinstead (pb) | 1-85937-138-8 | £9.99 |
| Berkshire Living Memories | 1-85937-332-1 | £14.99 | East London | 1-85937-080-2 | £14.99 |
| Black Country | 1-85937-497-2 | £12.99 | East Sussex (pb) | 1-85937-606-1 | £9.99 |
| Blackpool (pb) | 1-85937-393-3 | £9.99 | Eastbourne (pb) | 1-85937-399-2 | £9.99 |
| Bognor Regis (pb) | 1-85937-431-x | £9.99 | Edinburgh (pb) | 1-85937-193-0 | £8.99 |
| Bournemouth (pb) | 1-85937-545-6 | £9.99 | England In The 1880s | 1-85937-331-3 | £17.99 |
| Bradford (pb) | 1-85937-204-x | £9.99 | Essex - Second Selection | 1-85937-456-5 | £14.99 |
| Bridgend (pb) | 1-85937-386-0 | £7.99 | Essex (pb) | 1-85937-270-8 | £9.99 |
| Bridgwater (pb) | 1-85937-305-4 | £9.99 | Essex Coast | 1-85937-342-9 | £14.99 |
| Bridport (pb) | 1-85937-327-5 | £9.99 | Essex Living Memories | 1-85937-490-5 | £14.99 |
| Brighton (pb) | 1-85937-192-2 | £8.99 | Exeter | 1-85937-539-1 | £9.99 |
| Bristol (pb) | 1-85937-264-3 | £9.99 | Exmoor (pb) | 1-85937-608-8 | £9.99 |
| British Life A Century Ago (pb) | 1-85937-213-9 | £9.99 | Falmouth (pb) | 1-85937-594-4 | £9.99 |
| Buckinghamshire (pb) | 1-85937-200-7 | £9.99 | Folkestone (pb) | 1-85937-124-8 | £9.99 |
| Camberley (pb) | 1-85937-222-8 | £9.99 | Frome (pb) | 1-85937-317-8 | £9.99 |
| Cambridge (pb) | 1-85937-422-0 | £9.99 | Glamorgan | 1-85937-488-3 | £14.99 |
| Cambridgeshire (pb) | 1-85937-420-4 | £9.99 | Glasgow (pb) | 1-85937-190-6 | £9.99 |
| Cambridgeshire Villages | 1-85937-523-5 | £14.99 | Glastonbury (pb) | 1-85937-338-0 | £7.99 |
| Canals And Waterways (pb) | 1-85937-291-0 | £9.99 | Gloucester (pb) | 1-85937-232-5 | £9.99 |
| Canterbury Cathedral (pb) | 1-85937-179-5 | £9.99 | Gloucestershire (pb) | 1-85937-561-8 | £9.99 |
| Cardiff (pb) | 1-85937-093-4 | £9.99 | Great Yarmouth (pb) | 1-85937-426-3 | £9.99 |
| Carmarthenshire (pb) | 1-85937-604-5 | £9.99 | Greater Manchester (pb) | 1-85937-266-x | £9.99 |
| Chelmsford (pb) | 1-85937-310-0 | £9.99 | Guildford (pb) | 1-85937-410-7 | £9.99 |
| Cheltenham (pb) | 1-85937-095-0 | £9.99 | Hampshire (pb) | 1-85937-279-1 | £9.99 |
| Cheshire (pb) | 1-85937-271-6 | £9.99 | Harrogate (pb) | 1-85937-423-9 | £9.99 |
| Chester (pb) | 1-85937-382 8 | £9.99 | Hastings and Bexhill (pb) | 1-85937-131-0 | £9.99 |
| Chesterfield (pb) | 1-85937-378-x | £9.99 | Heart of Lancashire (pb) | 1-85937-197-3 | £9.99 |
| Chichester (pb) | 1-85937-228-7 | £9.99 | Helston (pb) | 1-85937-214-7 | £9.99 |
| Churches of East Cornwall (pb) | 1-85937-249-x | £9.99 | Hereford (pb) | 1-85937-175-2 | £9.99 |
| Churches of Hampshire (pb) | 1-85937-207-4 | £9.99 | Herefordshire (pb) | 1-85937-567-7 | £9.99 |
| Cinque Ports & Two Ancient Towns | 1-85937-492-1 | £14.99 | Herefordshire Living Memories | 1-85937-514-6 | £14.99 |
| Colchester (pb) | 1-85937-188-4 | £8.99 | Hertfordshire (pb) | 1-85937-247-3 | £9.99 |
| Cornwall (pb) | 1-85937-229-5 | £9.99 | Horsham (pb) | 1-85937-432-8 | £9.99 |
| Cornwall Living Memories | 1-85937-248-1 | £14.99 | Humberside (pb) | 1-85937-605-3 | £9.99 |
| Cotswolds (pb) | 1-85937-230-9 | £9.99 | Hythe, Romney Marsh, Ashford (pb) | 1-85937-256-2 | £9.99 |
| Cotswolds Living Memories | 1-85937-255-4 | £14.99 | Ipswich (pb) | 1-85937-424-7 | £9.99 |
| County Durham (pb) | 1-85937-398-4 | £9.99 | Isle of Man (pb) | 1-85937-268-6 | £9.99 |
| Croydon Living Memories (pb) | 1-85937-162-0 | £9.99 | Isle of Wight (pb) | 1-85937-429-8 | £9.99 |
| Cumbria (pb) | 1-85937-621-5 | £9.99 | Isle of Wight Living Memories | 1-85937-304-6 | £14.99 |
| Derby (pb) | 1-85937-367-4 | £9.99 | Kent (pb) | 1-85937-189-2 | £9.99 |
| Derbyshire (pb) | 1-85937-196-5 | £9.99 | Kent Living Memories(pb) | 1-85937-401-8 | £9.99 |
| Derbyshire Living Memories | 1-85937-330-5 | £14.99 | Kings Lynn (pb) | 1-85937-334-8 | £9.99 |

## Available from your local bookshop or from the publisher

# Frith Book Co Titles (continued)

| Title | ISBN | Price | Title | ISBN | Price |
|---|---|---|---|---|---|
| Lake District (pb) | 1-85937-275-9 | £9.99 | Sherborne (pb) | 1-85937-301-1 | £9.99 |
| Lancashire Living Memories | 1-85937-335-6 | £14.99 | Shrewsbury (pb) | 1-85937-325-9 | £9.99 |
| Lancaster, Morecambe, Heysham (pb) | 1-85937-233-3 | £9.99 | Shropshire (pb) | 1-85937-326-7 | £9.99 |
| Leeds (pb) | 1-85937-202-3 | £9.99 | Shropshire Living Memories | 1-85937-643-6 | £14.99 |
| Leicester (pb) | 1-85937-381-x | £9.99 | Somerset | 1-85937-153-1 | £14.99 |
| Leicestershire & Rutland Living Memories | 1-85937-500-6 | £12.99 | South Devon Coast | 1-85937-107-8 | £14.99 |
| Leicestershire (pb) | 1-85937-185-x | £9.99 | South Devon Living Memories (pb) | 1-85937-609-6 | £9.99 |
| Lighthouses | 1-85937-257-0 | £9.99 | South East London (pb) | 1-85937-263-5 | £9.99 |
| Lincoln (pb) | 1-85937-380-1 | £9.99 | South Somerset | 1-85937-318-6 | £14.99 |
| Lincolnshire (pb) | 1-85937-433-6 | £9.99 | South Wales | 1-85937-519-7 | £14.99 |
| Liverpool and Merseyside (pb) | 1-85937-234-1 | £9.99 | Southampton (pb) | 1-85937-427-1 | £9.99 |
| London (pb) | 1-85937-183-3 | £9.99 | Southend (pb) | 1-85937-313-5 | £9.99 |
| London Living Memories | 1-85937-454-9 | £14.99 | Southport (pb) | 1-85937-425-5 | £9.99 |
| Ludlow (pb) | 1-85937-176-0 | £9.99 | St Albans (pb) | 1-85937-341-0 | £9.99 |
| Luton (pb) | 1-85937-235-x | £9.99 | St Ives (pb) | 1-85937-415-8 | £9.99 |
| Maidenhead (pb) | 1-85937-339-9 | £9.99 | Stafford Living Memories (pb) | 1-85937-503-0 | £9.99 |
| Maidstone (pb) | 1-85937-391-7 | £9.99 | Staffordshire (pb) | 1-85937-308-9 | £9.99 |
| Manchester (pb) | 1-85937-198-1 | £9.99 | Stourbridge (pb) | 1-85937-530-8 | £9.99 |
| Marlborough (pb) | 1-85937-336-4 | £9.99 | Stratford upon Avon (pb) | 1-85937-388-7 | £9.99 |
| Middlesex | 1-85937-158-2 | £14.99 | Suffolk (pb) | 1-85937-221-x | £9.99 |
| Monmouthshire | 1-85937-532-4 | £14.99 | Suffolk Coast (pb) | 1-85937-610-x | £9.99 |
| New Forest (pb) | 1-85937-390-9 | £9.99 | Surrey (pb) | 1-85937-240-6 | £9.99 |
| Newark (pb) | 1-85937-366-6 | £9.99 | Surrey Living Memories | 1-85937-328-3 | £14.99 |
| Newport, Wales (pb) | 1-85937-258-9 | £9.99 | Sussex (pb) | 1-85937-184-1 | £9.99 |
| Newquay (pb) | 1-85937-421-2 | £9.99 | Sutton (pb) | 1-85937-337-2 | £9.99 |
| Norfolk (pb) | 1-85937-195-7 | £9.99 | Swansea (pb) | 1-85937-167-1 | £9.99 |
| Norfolk Broads | 1-85937-486-7 | £14.99 | Taunton (pb) | 1-85937-314-3 | £9.99 |
| Norfolk Living Memories (pb) | 1-85937-402-6 | £9.99 | Tees Valley & Cleveland (pb) | 1-85937-623-1 | £9.99 |
| North Buckinghamshire | 1-85937-626-6 | £14.99 | Teignmouth (pb) | 1-85937-370-4 | £7.99 |
| North Devon Living Memories | 1-85937-261-9 | £14.99 | Thanet (pb) | 1-85937-116-7 | £9.99 |
| North Hertfordshire | 1-85937-547-2 | £14.99 | Tiverton (pb) | 1-85937-178-7 | £9.99 |
| North London (pb) | 1-85937-403-4 | £9.99 | Torbay (pb) | 1-85937-597-9 | £9.99 |
| North Somerset | 1-85937-302-x | £14.99 | Truro (pb) | 1-85937-598-7 | £9.99 |
| North Wales (pb) | 1-85937-298-8 | £9.99 | Victorian & Edwardian Dorset (pb) | 1-85937-254-6 | £14.99 |
| North Yorkshire (pb) | 1-85937-236-8 | £9.99 | Victorian & Edwardian Kent (pb) | 1-85937-624-X | £9.99 |
| Northamptonshire Living Memories | 1-85937-529-4 | £14.99 | Victorian & Edwardian Maritime Album (pb) | 1-85937-622-3 | £9.99 |
| Northamptonshire | 1-85937-150-7 | £14.99 | Victorian and Edwardian Sussex (pb) | 1-85937-625-8 | £9.99 |
| Northumberland Tyne & Wear (pb) | 1-85937-281-3 | £9.99 | Villages of Devon (pb) | 1-85937-293-7 | £9.99 |
| Northumberland | 1-85937-522-7 | £14.99 | Villages of Kent (pb) | 1-85937-294-5 | £9.99 |
| Norwich (pb) | 1-85937-194-9 | £8.99 | Villages of Sussex (pb) | 1-85937-295-3 | £9.99 |
| Nottingham (pb) | 1-85937-324-0 | £9.99 | Warrington (pb) | 1-85937-507-3 | £9.99 |
| Nottinghamshire (pb) | 1-85937-187-6 | £9.99 | Warwick (pb) | 1-85937-518-9 | £9.99 |
| Oxford (pb) | 1-85937-411-5 | £9.99 | Warwickshire (pb) | 1-85937-203-1 | £9.99 |
| Oxfordshire (pb) | 1-85937-430-1 | £9.99 | Welsh Castles (pb) | 1-85937-322-4 | £9.99 |
| Oxfordshire Living Memories | 1-85937-525-1 | £14.99 | West Midlands (pb) | 1-85937-289-9 | £9.99 |
| Paignton (pb) | 1-85937-374-7 | £7.99 | West Sussex (pb) | 1-85937-607-x | £9.99 |
| Peak District (pb) | 1-85937-280-5 | £9.99 | West Yorkshire (pb) | 1-85937-201-5 | £9.99 |
| Pembrokeshire | 1-85937-262-7 | £14.99 | Weston Super Mare (pb) | 1-85937-306-2 | £9.99 |
| Penzance (pb) | 1-85937-595-2 | £9.99 | Weymouth (pb) | 1-85937-209-0 | £9.99 |
| Peterborough (pb) | 1-85937-219-8 | £9.99 | Wiltshire (pb) | 1-85937-277-5 | £9.99 |
| Picturesque Harbours | 1-85937-208-2 | £14.99 | Wiltshire Churches (pb) | 1-85937-171-x | £9.99 |
| Piers | 1-85937-237-6 | £17.99 | Wiltshire Living Memories (pb) | 1-85937-396-8 | £9.99 |
| Plymouth (pb) | 1-85937-389-5 | £9.99 | Winchester (pb) | 1-85937-428-x | £9.99 |
| Poole & Sandbanks (pb) | 1-85937-251-1 | £9.99 | Windsor (pb) | 1-85937-333-x | £9.99 |
| Preston (pb) | 1-85937-212-0 | £9.99 | Wokingham & Bracknell (pb) | 1-85937-329-1 | £9.99 |
| Reading (pb) | 1-85937-238-4 | £9.99 | Woodbridge (pb) | 1-85937-498-0 | £9.99 |
| Redhill to Reigate (pb) | 1-85937-596-0 | £9.99 | Worcester (pb) | 1-85937-165-5 | £9.99 |
| Ringwood (pb) | 1-85937-384-4 | £7.99 | Worcestershire Living Memories | 1-85937-489-1 | £14.99 |
| Romford (pb) | 1-85937-319-4 | £9.99 | Worcestershire | 1-85937-152-3 | £14.99 |
| Royal Tunbridge Wells (pb) | 1-85937-504-9 | £9.99 | York (pb) | 1-85937-199-x | £9.99 |
| Salisbury (pb) | 1-85937-239-2 | £9.99 | Yorkshire (pb) | 1-85937-186-8 | £9.99 |
| Scarborough (pb) | 1-85937-379-8 | £9.99 | Yorkshire Coastal Memories | 1-85937-506-5 | £14.99 |
| Sevenoaks and Tonbridge (pb) | 1-85937-392-5 | £9.99 | Yorkshire Dales | 1-85937-502-2 | £14.99 |
| Sheffield & South Yorks (pb) | 1-85937-267-8 | £9.99 | Yorkshire Living Memories (pb) | 1-85937-397-6 | £9.99 |

**See Frith books on the internet at www.francisfrith.co.uk**

# FRITH PRODUCTS & SERVICES

Francis Frith would doubtless be pleased to know that the pioneering publishing venture he started in 1860 still continues today. Over a hundred and forty years later, The Francis Frith Collection continues in the same innovative tradition and is now one of the foremost publishers of vintage photographs in the world. Some of the current activities include:

### Interior Decoration

Today Frith's photographs can be seen framed and as giant wall murals in thousands of pubs, restaurants, hotels, banks, retail stores and other public buildings throughout the country. In every case they enhance the unique local atmosphere of the places they depict and provide reminders of gentler days in an increasingly busy and frenetic world.

### Product Promotions

Frith products are used by many major companies to promote the sales of their own products or to reinforce their own history and heritage. Frith promotions have been used by Hovis bread, Courage beers, Scots Porage Oats, Colman's mustard, Cadbury's foods, Mellow Birds coffee, Dunhill pipe tobacco, Guinness, and Bulmer's Cider.

### Genealogy and Family History

As the interest in family history and roots grows world-wide, more and more people are turning to Frith's photographs of Great Britain for images of the towns, villages and streets where their ancestors lived; and, of course, photographs of the churches and chapels where their ancestors were christened, married and buried are an essential part of every genealogy tree and family album.

### Frith Products

All Frith photographs are available Framed or just as Mounted Prints and Posters (size 23 x 16 inches). These may be ordered from the address below. From time to time other products - Address Books, Calendars, Table Mats, etc - are available.

### The Internet

Already fifty thousand Frith photographs can be viewed and purchased on the internet through the Frith websites and a myriad of partner sites.

For more detailed information on Frith companies and products, look at these sites:

www.francisfrith.co.uk
www.francisfrith.com
*(for North American visitors)*

---

See the complete list of Frith Books at:

*www.francisfrith.co.uk*

This web site is regularly updated with the latest list of publications from the Frith Book Company. If you wish to buy books relating to another part of the country that your local bookshop does not stock, you may purchase on-line.

---

*For further information, trade, or author enquiries please contact us at the address below:*
**The Francis Frith Collection, Frith's Barn, Teffont, Salisbury, Wiltshire, England SP3 5QP.**
Tel: +44 (0)1722 716 376  Fax: +44 (0)1722 716 881   Email: sales@francisfrith.co.uk

## See Frith books on the internet at www.francisfrith.co.uk

# FREE MOUNTED PRINT

**Mounted Print**
*Overall size 14 x 11 inches*

**Fill in and cut out this voucher and return**
*it with your remittance for £2.25 (to cover postage and handling). Offer valid for delivery to UK addresses only.*

**Choose any photograph included in this book.**
*Your SEPIA print will be A4 in size. It will be mounted in a cream mount with a burgundy rule line (overall size 14 x 11 inches).*

**Order additional Mounted Prints at HALF PRICE (only £7.49 each*)**
If you would like to order more Frith prints from this book, possibly as gifts for friends and family, you can buy them at half price (with no additional postage and handling costs).

**Have your Mounted Prints framed**
For an extra £14.95 per print* you can have your mounted print(s) framed in an elegant polished wood and gilt moulding, overall size 16 x 13 inches (no additional postage and handling required).

---

**\* IMPORTANT!**

**These special prices are only available if you order at the same time as you order your free mounted print. You must use the ORIGINAL VOUCHER on this page (no copies permitted). We can only despatch to one address.**

---

*Send completed Voucher form to:*
**The Francis Frith Collection, Frith's Barn, Teffont, Salisbury, Wiltshire SP3 5QP**

## CHOOSE ANY IMAGE FROM THIS BOOK

*Voucher* for **FREE** and Reduced Price Frith Prints

*Please do not photocopy this voucher. Only the original is valid, so please fill it in, cut it out and return it to us with your order.*

| Picture ref no | Page no | Qty | Mounted @ £7.49 | Framed + £14.95 | Total Cost |
|---|---|---|---|---|---|
| | | 1 | Free of charge* | £ | £ |
| | | | £7.49 | £ | £ |
| | | | £7.49 | £ | £ |
| | | | £7.49 | £ | £ |
| | | | £7.49 | £ | £ |
| | | | £7.49 | £ | £ |
| *Please allow 28 days for delivery* | | | * Post & handling (UK) | | £2.25 |
| | | | **Total Order Cost** | | £ |

Title of this book . . . . . . . . . . . . . . . . . . . . . .

I enclose a cheque/postal order for £ . . . . . . . . . .
made payable to 'The Francis Frith Collection'

OR please debit my Mastercard / Visa / Switch / Amex card
*(credit cards please on all overseas orders),* details below

Card Number

Issue No (Switch only)          Valid from (Amex/Switch)

Expires          Signature

Name  Mr/Mrs/Ms . . . . . . . . . . . . . . . . . . . . . .
Address . . . . . . . . . . . . . . . . . . . . . . . . . . . .
. . . . . . . . . . . . . . . . . . . . . . . . . . . . . . . . .
. . . . . . . . . . . . . . . . . . . . . . . . . . . . . . . . .
. . . . . . . . . . . . . . . . . . . . Postcode . . . . . . . .
Daytime Tel No . . . . . . . . . . . . . . . . . . . . . . .
Email . . . . . . . . . . . . . . . . . . . . . . . . . . . . . .

Valid to 31/12/05

Free Print – see overleaf

**Would you like to find out more about Francis Frith?**

We have recently recruited some entertaining speakers who are happy to visit local groups, clubs and societies to give an illustrated talk documenting Frith's travels and photographs. If you are a member of such a group and are interested in hosting a presentation, we would love to hear from you.

Our speakers bring with them a small selection of our local town and county books, together with sample prints. They are happy to take orders. A small proportion of the order value is donated to the group who have hosted the presentation. The talks are therefore an excellent way of fundraising for small groups and societies.

**Can you help us with information about any of the Frith photographs in this book?**

We are gradually compiling an historical record for each of the photographs in the Frith archive. It is always fascinating to find out the names of the people shown in the pictures, as well as insights into the shops, buildings and other features depicted.

If you recognize anyone in the photographs in this book, or if you have information not already included in the author's caption, do let us know. We would love to hear from you, and will try to publish it in future books or articles.

**Our production team**

Frith books are produced by a small dedicated team at offices in the converted Grade II listed 18th-century barn at Teffont near Salisbury, illustrated above. Most have worked with the Frith Collection for many years. All have in common one quality: they have a passion for the Frith Collection. The team is constantly expanding, but currently includes:

Jason Buck, John Buck, Ruth Butler, Heather Crisp, David Davies, Isobel Hall, Julian Hight, Peter Horne, James Kinnear, Karen Kinnear, Tina Leary, Stuart Login, Amanda Lowe, David Marsh, Sue Molloy, Kate Rotondetto, Dean Scource, Eliza Sackett, Terence Sackett, Sandra Sampson, Adrian Sanders, Sandra Sanger, Julia Skinner, Claire Tarrier, Lewis Taylor, Shelley Tolcher and Lorraine Tuck.